SACRED SILENCE

SACRED SILENCE

Meditations for Healing and Growth

GORDON ROJO

Deep Healing Meditations LLC

Contents

Acknowledgement

For my ancestors, friends, and all the people who love me. You inspire me to love harder and dig deeper.

-Gordon

Guided Audio Access

Scan the above QR code with your phone, and it will take you to the link-tree that contains all book resources. The guided audio is a tremendous aid, whether you are a beginner or an expert when it comes to meditation. Hearing someone else's voice allows you to sit back and experience the content without getting as easily derailed. Make use of this resource as frequently as you see fit.

I hope this gift serves you well!

Preface

This body of work is a collection of years worth of stories and meditations that have led to profound healing in both myself and others. Everything you are going to read is true—as it actually happened. Every meditation is transcribed from meditations that I consider the most potent of what I use and teach.

Many of the tools in this book are inspired by a fusion of philosophies ranging from Buddhism, Qi Gong, yoga, and more. These long-standing traditions provided the paint and canvas for me to create these unique meditations.

The meditations are inspired by others from different spiritual and philosophical paths, so some meditations may remind you of others you've done. Although they are similar, these meditations are adapted from personal deep experiences that can be transferred to a reader.

Though I transcribed them, it would be inaccurate for me to claim that I created them. Rather, they were channeled through me and I experienced them for the first time similar to how I hope you will: with an open heart and a ready spirit.

When reading this book, take everything at face value and see how it sits with you. Something may not resonate now, but could make more sense down the line. The meditations are for your use and are intended to be adapted for your own practice. If something feels good, then do it! If it doesn't, leave it behind.

Ultimately, the spiritual journey is a personal one. This just so happens to be mine, and the tools that have worked for myself and others along the way. Take from it what you can, and build upon it.

This is your practice, so enjoy it!

Diagrams

The following diagrams are to help you navigate the text in the book a little bit easier. The Dhyana mudra, understanding where the chakras are in the body (details on them can be found in chapter 5), and breathing deeply are all crucial to getting the full experience with the meditations in the book.

Dhyana Mudra

This mudra is one of the easiest, least distracting mudras to use that allows you to build up energy throughout the body. Think of your fingers as wires—using mudras helps you focus on emphasizing certain kinds of energy, while leaving behind others.

For those who identify with feminine energy, place your right hand on top facing up. For those who identify with masculine energy, face your left hand on top facing up.

The Seven Chakras

Above are the seven chakras and where they are located in your body, starting from the first chakra at the base of your spine all the way up to the seventh chakra located at the very top of your head. An in-depth explanation of these energy centers can be found in

Chapter 5, but this diagram will be a reference point to see where exactly they land in the body.

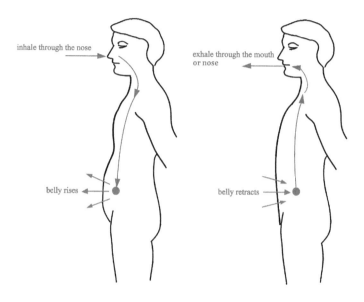

inhale through the nose

exhale through the mouth or nose

belly rises

belly retracts

How to Breathe Deeply

Above is a simple diagram on how to breathe deeply using your diaphragm. In meditation, this kind of breathing is particularly useful for relaxation and becoming grounded in the body. It can be done from any position, whether you are laying down or sitting up. Practice this breathing this way a few times before using it in meditation. If you don't have experience with diaphragm breathing already, it can be a bit challenging at first to get the hang of.

I

Miracles are Normal

The year was 2017, and boy was I lost. It was a hot summer day, and I was fatigued from walking 8-10 hours per day for the last week. I was on a journey to find a sweet, beautiful woman named Lucia.

After our magical weekend together full of love in the country-side of Spain, we had to part ways all too quickly. Some friends and I went with her to the train station and saw her off on her way back home. Holding back tears, I said goodbye... but she did something that surprised me. As she was stepping onto the train, she turned around and gave me a note with a location on it: Playa de Lima, and simply said "Come find me."

Now, imagine being in my shoes. I connected deeper with this beautiful, radiant, magical goddess of a woman than I've ever con-nected with anyone in my life. It felt as though the universe had aligned every detail of our meeting as to emphasize our role to come in one another's life.

So, naturally, I set out on my way, having my new friends drop me off on the Camino de Santiago as a means to travel north through the country. I was no stranger to being alone, seeing that I had bought my one-way ticket to Spain and set out on my journey two-and-a-half months ago... a time span that felt like eons when compared to how I was living at home. Every moment since arriving in Spain was so dense and full of wonder.

Yet there I was, having successfully crossed the country by foot for the last week, somewhere within 15 kilometers of Lucia, when everything died.

My phone that I was using as a map was dead, my solar powered chargers were no longer working, and I had used the last means of public transportation to get as close as I could to the fabled Playa de Limas.

All I had left to use for navigation was a cheap compass and a yearning heart.

I thought to myself, "I know she's north-west from where I am, and by the water... Should be easy to find a beach, right?"

I could not have been more wrong. I spent hours trying to walk north-west but the winding mountain roads made it impossible to walk in one single direction. I would get thrown off course, try to correct, get thrown off course, and try to correct again. Within a few short hours not only was I completely lost, but I had absolutely no way of getting back to where I was originally. With few other options, I asked for divine help.

I prayed to the universe and said, "God, if I'm walking in the direction of Lucia please show me 11's on the license plates of the cars I pass. If I'm headed down a wrong street, show me 10's and 12's." I was asking for synchronicities to guide the way.

It's useful to explain here that Synchronicities, or meaningful co-incidences/signs from the universe, can come in an infinite number of forms. The object (or number) that they appear on is not impor-tant—the way you know what you're viewing is a synchronicity is by the way you feel. It is as though you're looking at something nearly impossible or highly unlikely, and yet it's there. Initially they will blow your mind, and eventually they become a part of your everyday experience as you learn how to navigate the world around you. Like tarot cards or anything of the sort, sometimes when you ask for a divine synchronicity, you'll get one.

For me, the chance alone of seeing Lucia again was enough to roll the dice. It may have been a long shot, but my prayer was all I had left. Armed with a desperate plea to the universe, I continued walking with seeming aimlessness through the Spanish mountain roads.

"11, ok good."

"12, alright I had better go the other way."

"Another 11, I think this is the right way."

"A fork in the road... that license plate has a 10 on it, let's try the other direction."

After another hour or two of this, I noticed the sun was coming closer to setting. I had about two more hours of daylight before things really got dark, and it would be unlikely that I could find Lucia on the beach.

It was right around this time that I thought to myself, "Alright. I might really be screwed now."

As I thought this to myself, I saw a rickety street sign that happened to be at the end of the street I was standing on, resting at a 45° angle. Out of sheer curiousness, I walked up to it to see where such an out-of-place street sign could lead. Its crookedness stuck out against it's surroundings like a sore thumb, seeing that every other street sign was perfectly straight. When I got close enough to read it, however, I was in total disbelief.

It read Playa de Lima.

Hours of walking, following a compass, getting lost, and asking desperately for signs via the license plates around in the absence of other human beings, I had found my beach. The sign was crooked at an angle because the road itself lead straight down the mountain.

As I examined the beach below, I realized that there was absolutely no way I could have found it on my own.

First of all, I got so disoriented trying to walk north-west that I didn't even realize I had been walking up a mountain. I had started my walk that day at sea level, and being so high up was a surprise to say the least. Even more amazingly, Playa de Lima is a tiny beach nestled in a mountain valley of which is impossible to see, unless you are looking at it from directly above. As the shock of finding this secret beach began to settle into my body, I hiked down the steep mountain road to try and find Lucia while I still had the daylight to do so. When I arrived at the bottom, I saw that the little road dumped directly into the coarse dark brown sand and the beach extended both to the left and the right.

As I stood there deciding which direction to search first, I hear "RED!" and turn to my right to find Lucia running towards me topless, with a wide grin and joyous stride.

In this moment, it felt as though time stood still. Everything had just become real. I had spent the last 6 days crossing the country by foot, rain or shine, for 8-10 hours a day. I had run out of food, water, and money at different points during my trek, surviving off of the berries and apples that grew along the trail for travelers. I had gotten completely lost in a town I had never been in, and was guided by the mysterious force of the universe via something as trivial as license plates to find my love. It had all happened and seeing Lucia running towards me into my arms was living proof.

The moment her sweet kisses landed against my cheek and lips, I was instantly shot back into the moment I was in. She burst with excitement, saying "I could feel you were here!"

We found a spot for us to set up my hammock in the willow trees and placed her tent in a grove of trees where it would be out of sight. We spent the rest of the day laughing, talking about life, and pondering the wonders of love as twilight settled onto the beach.

It felt as though the world stopped, and everything in existence brought us together to meet once more in an evening filled with unsuspected magic.

And though I was focused on Lucia, something was planted deep in my soul that day. Something beyond either one of us that lingered in my mind for years to come: the power of the universe, its guidance, and the appearance of miracles. They really did exist, and I now had definitive proof.

I share this story with you as an example of real, powerful events that can happen when we connect with ourselves and the world around us. These kinds of miracles and answering of prayers can happen to anyone, but the more one builds upon themselves through a practice of meditation (or yoga, art, or anything of the like) the more prone they become to these kinds of events. Though you will likely find some kind of all-encompassing presence in deeper meditations (some call it God, Allah, Jah, Yahweh, divine, etc.) a belief in a higher power is not required. Much less is it required to name or understand this force that seems to sew everything together. It is our connection through our heart that connects us to the world, and one of the most effective ways of exploring it is through meditation. You will find through meditation that there is no real limit to your heart or anything else for that matter, and miracles work in the same way that your hand levitates if you raise your arm.

You do not consider your floating hand a miracle because you understand the mechanics;

it only takes our arm to lift it. The same works with divine intervention: these moments are not so unobtainable once we understand the forces of the universe at play, and submit ourselves to them.

Though such direct help does not come every day, the presence that can move objects and generate miracles is with you every day. If you are to change your life, witness miracles, and go through substantial healing, then you must start from within.

The following meditations in this chapter aim to do just that. They are meditations to help start you along the path or aid you if you already have a practice. They may take time for you to develop. I recommend trying each one at least twice before you leave it for another one and seeing if you can get to a state of relaxation while doing so. Put on some meditation music, dim the lights, and give yourself the space to feel what comes up.

Feel Your Body

Begin with an optional 10-15 minutes of stretching your body in any areas that feel tight, while still hitting as much of the rest of the body as you can. This is not a workout, so make sure to stay relaxed and do what feels good for you today.

Once stretched out, sit down cross-legged with your hands in whatever position is comfortable. Begin by taking 5-10 slow deep breaths.

Relax the body, and once you feel calm, begin focusing on the sensations in both of your feet. Do not move or wiggle them, but simply feel them.

When you can isolate this region specifically and feel how it feels, move up to the calves and repeat. Use your focus and attention to specifically feel your calves until you can comfortably do so without much effort.

Continue repeating this process until you have isolated each part of the body from the bottom up.

Conclude by feeling the sensations in your entire body all at once. Stay in this space and listen to your body for a while, feeling any emotions that arise.

Allow the sensations you feel to melt into your emotions, and any energy you feel in the body. Let every sensation and stimuli become one experience that you simply observe.

When you feel you're ready, drift back into your body and waking consciousness, engaging your 5 senses before opening your eyes. You can do this by rubbing your thumb on your fingertips, inviting movement into your spine, or noticing the sounds and smells around you.

Transformative Gardening

Using the Dhyana mudra (page x) sit upright and begin by taking slow, deep breaths, focusing your attention inward.

Feel the movement of your breath as it enters and leaves your body. Take a few moments to let go of the day, and release any thoughts that may be lingering in your mind back to the earth.

Focus on deepening your breath further, and relax.

Once you are relaxed and in meditation, begin visualizing that your whole body is like soil, ready to support any thought that you plant in it.

Make the garden of your consciousness something that feels beautiful, and water the thoughts you want to grow with your intention.

What plants/thoughts are already planted in your garden? What plants would you like to keep?

What plants would you like to weed out?

When you find a plant or thought that no longer serves you, use your breath to dig it out of the soil and let it go. Replace this thought with one you'd like to grow in its place, and visualize the thought as a beautiful plant or flower.

Stay here for a while admiring your garden and making it what you like.

When you're ready to end the meditation, begin to become aware again of your bodily sensations and how you physically feel in this moment. Feel your breath expanding your chest.

Once you're re-grounded (consciously connected to the body), open your eyes and reflect.

2

Connecting with Meditation

"Man, I should really start meditating."

"I need to meditate more."

"I can't sit still and meditate like that, I don't get how you do that!"

Sound familiar? Are these phrases that you have said yourself? I cannot tell you how many times I've heard these when I tell people I guide meditations, and every time I hear it, I am always surprised by their answer. Here's why:

Meditation is not sitting still silently with no thoughts in your brain.

Or at least it doesn't have to be in order to receive healing and growth. Meditation in the sense I'm speaking of is more about following a feeling—whether it be an emotion, physical discomfort, the breath, or a gut/intuitive feeling (more on that later). This is the reason why Tai Qi, Yoga, dancing, and other movement-based practices can be just as powerful as meditation. You are still actively learning about yourself, and what it means to listen to something *other than your mind.*

That's the secret to meditation. In order to "shut off your mind" you are not actually shutting it off yourself. You cannot will the mind into silence—to try and do so would be counterproductive. You are training your awareness to be able to be stimulated, or listen to, other forms of sensation in the body and mind. When you are able to focus your attention on a bodily sensation such as a yoga pose, or an emotion you want to bring more into your life, you are showing your awareness what can capture your attention. Your body, being an amazing vehicle of stimulation, will respond during meditation and begin to give you more of that.

The problem that we face is not that we think too much, but rather we attach our identity to these thoughts. You may believe that you are the sum of your thoughts, when in reality you are the phenomenon that interprets them.

Because at some level we may believe our thoughts are the definition of who we are, we become immensely stimulated by them and thus pay them more attention than other sensations.

"I can't believe I'm considering this, I'm a terrible person!"
or
"I think I am x, y, or z, and therefore should act as x, y, or z would act."

When we give a single stimuli such as thought all of our attention, we don't leave room for other sensations to enter our awareness. Maybe you are shocked by your angry thoughts, rather than remembering that you haven't eaten in a few hours and your stomach is aching. Or maybe you are overly-invested on the thought you just had of driving your car off of the side of the road, rather than the fact you don't feel comfortable in the place that you're driving to. In both examples, the other feelings/sensations are just as relevant to understanding the situation and your role in it, yet these feelings are often undermined by the volume of our thoughts.

One way to deal with these discrepancies is to breathe into them. By simply relaxing, seeing what you're resisting, and feeling it, you're able to ease the tension and move past it. Even more noteworthy, you're able to catch glimpses of what it could be rooted in and heal it all together.

When you begin to focus on the other sensations at play inside of you (namely bodily sensations, intuitive feelings, emotions, etc.) you gain a level of access to yourself previously unknowable from just the context of your thoughts. All of your feelings and sensations provide the context that paints your picture of reality, mind included. The purpose of meditation is not to force the mind into silent submission, but instead elevate your awareness of your other feelings so the mind naturally falls to the wayside, becoming a tool to be used as needed.

It is with this perspective of meditation that we will continue through the chapters of the book. This is the kind of meditation that brings you closer to you—all of you.

That itself is enough of a reason to pursue meditation. To understand yourself means understanding how to make your heart happy and your life vibrant.

It's about following the sensations and feelings in your being and seeing where they lead you. Will it take practice to focus on your feelings instead of just your thoughts? Absolutely. Will it be worth it? Most definitely.

Remain consistent, try meditating at least once a day, and you'll begin seeing results. You'll feel more lucid, aware, and in tune with your feelings. Most of all, you'll find a kind of peace that you may be encountering for the first time.

Getting to Know Yourself

Begin with slow, deep breathing that allows you to feel comfortable and sink deeply within yourself. This can take as long as necessary, there is no rush.

When ready, introduce yourself to your inner, deeper, truest self as if you've never met before. Begin asking questions to your inner self that you'd normally ask others to know them on a deeper level:

"What are your passions?"
"What is troubling you?"
"What do you care most about?"
"What do you love?"
"What is it that you want?"

And so on. Allow your inner-self to speak back to you through feelings. If you feel called, ask for their opinion on something that has been on your mind. Pay close attention to your feelings during this process, especially when answering back to the questions.

Make sure to talk to them as if you're just meeting them for the first time, as though they're a different consciousness with different knowledge that you may not know.

Once you feel complete, ground yourself by feeling your body and engaging your senses before opening your eyes. You can do this by rubbing your thumb on your fingertips, inviting movement into your spine, or noticing the sounds around you.

Breathing with the Earth

This meditation can be done sitting up in a cross-legged position, standing, or lying down. Begin by simply breathing. Feel the air coming in and out of your body, filling you with energy and ease.

Allow yourself to notice any tension in your body, and continue to relax even deeper as you direct your breath to these areas of tension.

Place both hands towards or on the ground. Breathe as if you are inhaling the energy coming from the ground below you. Exhale in the same fashion; from your hands directly back into the earth.

Once you're comfortable doing this, imagine you're sitting on top of a perfectly clear mirror with your reflection beneath you. Your hands are touching the hands of your reflection, your seat resting upon the seat of your reflection.

Imagine this second self to be your ideal self, full of energy and supporting you from the bottom. They can give you what you need in the moment you need it—whether it be energy, compassion, or love.

They are everything you wish to be, giving you energy in abundance.

Connect with this second self as long as you'd like, continuing to gently breathe into each other's hands.

Once you feel ready, gently focus on the feeling of your physical body and energy, slowly coming back to yourself before you open your eyes.

Grounding Roots

For this meditation, you'll be seated in an upright position, Dhyana mudra (page x), legs crossed.

Start by breathing in and out slowly through the nose. Bring energy peacefully up the spine on the in-breath, and back down on the out-breath.

Once you're relaxed and your energy is flowing (or you can at least visualize it), begin to feel your body on just the skin level. While staying still, feel the entirety of your external body, and relax into it.

Come to peace here, allowing yourself to relax further, and continuing to breathe. Stay here for a while, and when you're ready, visualize tree roots extending out from the bottom of your spine connecting you deeply with the earth below you.

Imagine these roots bringing energy up from the earth below to nourish you, allowing you to flourish, giving you energy where you need it most.

Stay here as long as feels good. When you feel complete, simply return to your bodily sensations and continue about your day.

3

Getting to Know Yourself

Before we can dive into this chapter, there is one major fact that must be established:

Knowing yourself is not linear. You change all of the time.

We live in a society that pushes us to find a career, a stable partner to have children with, and one home to live in until we retire. This ethos is founded upon one major myth that we have foolishly clung to: that we are static beings, and once we find ourselves, we know who we are and what we want to do. The fact is, we are changing constantly as we take in new information and grow in unexpected ways.

Take your own life for example. I'm willing to bet that you've had a partner or friend that you thought would be in your life forever, and yet somehow time, conflict, or circumstance wedged between the two of you and the nature of the relationship changed. It's not that you did not love them fully when you first set your heart onto them, but rather as you both grew the nature of the relationship had to readjust—sometimes in ways that retain the relationship, sometimes not. The important elements are not what sticks around, but rather who you become.

Though changes in relationships can usually be seen overtime, ones relationship with themselves is open to change much more rapidly. One week you could be full of conviction and know exactly where you stand in the universe and what you want to do, and the next week you could be writhing in the existential chaos of having not the slightest clue of who you are and what to make of your life. Although it may not be readily understood by more conservative groups or society, *this is normal.* Even better than normal, this can be a positive thing when seen through to its transformative ending.

According to Suzy Ross, author of *The Map to Wholeness*, this state of watching your old desires and identity fade away is known as the Return phase, the fourth of thirteen phases on the path to transformation. It is a time often in conjunction with a change in our lives, whether that change be internal or external. Although this unknowingness of who you are can be quite unsettling, there is some refuge in knowing that you're experiencing it because you're outgrowing old habits and ways of thinking, and are rapidly aligning yourself towards a new, more full reality.

But why is it that we can be so sure of a decision, and be pulling back a few weeks later? Aside from growth, there's another reason for this that I break down as the three selves.

In each of us, we have three levels of consciousness: *lower self, middle self, and higher self.* Each self performs a different function, and their definition is similar in some ways to Freud's Personality Theory, as well as the Hawaiian spiritual belief of the Three Selves of Huna. Here's my summary of each of the three selves:

<u>Lower Self</u>: This self is responsible for your earthly desires,

impulses, cravings, and physical safety. It's associated with the 1st and 2nd chakra (don't worry if you don't know what this means, it will be discussed in chapter 5). The part of you that craves coffee, for example, is your lower self.

Middle Self: The Middle Self is the glue between your higher and lower self, and the one that actually engages with your day-to-day activities here on Earth. It's associated with our 3rd, 4th, and 5th chakra. If you're healthy and stable, you likely spend most of your time operating at this level of consciousness. This is the part of you that actually makes the plan to go to your favorite coffee shop and get a cup of coffee.

Higher Self: This self is responsible for navigating you through the unseen parts of your world. This state of consciousness can appear in many ways, but all usually seem elusive: a gut feeling, a stray but significant thought, feeling like you know or recognize something that you otherwise would not, feelings of deep joy or peace, and much more. Your Higher Self can interact with you through any of your seven chakras, however it can especially be found in the 6th and 7th chakras when one has a consistent practice of mindfulness. In the example given with the other selves, the Higher Self is the part of you that tells you it's important to go to a coffee shop today instead of brewing your own—although you may have no tangible reason as to why (yet).

In one form or another, it's likely you've experienced the distinct differences in these selves although you may not have labeled them as such. Perhaps your Lower Self has felt the urge to snap back at someone who was unkind to you, but your Middle Self negotiated with it to bite your tongue. Or maybe you've had a gut feeling come from your Higher Self, but your Middle Self could not reason out a logical reason to follow the feeling and went the other way. Beginning to understand these different levels of consciousness inside of you helps you make sense of your sometimes conflicting feelings, as well as get to know who you are as a whole. In order to dive deeper, it's important to put these selves into context.

The names Higher, Middle, and Lower Self are a bit of a misnomer. Naturally, when we hear these words, we instinctively assume that the Higher Self is best and where we want to be, with the Lower Self being a poor decision maker and to be avoided where possible. This is made worse by the widespread idea that impulsive decisions are destructive and do not lead to desirable outcomes. With these myths recognized, I think it's time we give the Lower Self the credit it deserves.

The Lower Self is responsible for keeping you safe and showing you what you enjoy here on Earth. It teaches you how to find pleasure in your surroundings, and give you a life that you are delighted to partake in. Sometimes the Lower Self acts in predictable ways, like not wanting to say goodbye to a lover when it's time to go, or craving chocolate when you're on a diet. But other times the Lower Self acts in ways that are harder to plot on a chart, and even harder to grasp in the moment they are happening. By its very nature, the Lower Self is impulsive.

But being impulsive is not a plague of the Lower Self—rather it's a genius quality. Being impulsive is more often than not the catalyst to some of the biggest changes in our lives, and it is this uncomfortable state of change that likely earned the Lower Self its reputation. Impulsive decisions do not bring with them destruction, but rather chaos. Usually, if you're lucky, the chaos brought from an impulsive decision is mild and at best entertaining. Although great stories come out of the executive decisions made by the Lower Self in an impulsive state, having fun is not the function that chaos serves towards our growth. The reason why impulsion is a gift is because *a state of chaos breeds new possibilities and realities that would not otherwise be possible.*

Consider for a moment the last time your life was in shambles. Some kind of life event likely spurred this state into action, leaving you to figure out what to do next. Whether it was generated by an impulse or something outside of you is not so important. What is important is that this phase of your life likely pushed you way outside of your comfort zone, allowing you to step into a more expanded version of yourself. Maybe you acquired a new skill, became better at setting boundaries, or discovered a new passion or sense of purpose. If nothing else, maybe it gave you the gift of deepening your compassion and resilience. The gifts these phases can bring would not be possible without the catalyst of chaos.

It is true, however, that prolonged chaos can be destructive. Impulses and the chaos that they bring can only be constructive if they happen at precise, short bursts. The Lower Self uses impulse to create fresh, fertile grounds for a new life to grow—however, due to its nature it cannot feed and sustain these opportunities. That is where the Middle Self comes in.

After the storm of chaos brewed by the Lower Self is complete, the Middle Self comes in to assess what steps can be taken next. Having new and infinite possibilities for action is great, but they don't mean much unless tangible action is taken. The Middle Self is responsible for overseeing this action-taking process, where a selection is made on how to proceed in organizing your life again—maybe with a pointer or two coming from the Higher Self.

The actions carried out by your Middle Self are what give you confidence, expertise, and wisdom. It is the part of yourself that takes full advantage of the opportunity to be human, negotiating between the Higher and Lower Selves to maintain both satisfaction and the highest possible level of growth for yourself as a whole.

Usually, this is where we will spend most of our time in our lives. For some people, there is an over-focus on trying to access the Higher Self for wisdom and insight. The truth is, however, that it is your Middle Self that *creates* wisdom. Because it is situated between your immediate safety and desires, as well as your intuition and psychic components, it creates new patterns of reality that haven't existed before. In creating new situations and navigating them, you are able to take the lessons you learned from one situation and apply them to the rest of your life. This, in its essence, is the function of wisdom, and the foundation of where the Middle Self operates.

The Higher Self carries out a much different function that is elusive by its very nature. The Higher Self is the part of you that is connected to everything around you in a very direct way. It often produces intuitive and psychic feelings: "don't go here," "trust them," "so-and-so is close by." It governs your intuitive and psychic senses, although you may not immediately recognize it as such. Maybe you have taken one look at someone and knew they had loving intentions in their heart, or that they were emotionally hurting. The feelings generated when you look someone in the eye usually come from your Higher Self.

You can tell when the information you're receiving is coming from your Higher Self by the nature of the information and its ac-companied feeling. Whether you have a feeling of a wave of clarity washing over you, or an immediate clench in your stomach or neck, the information received usually follows a pattern of having very little or no connection with what you would normally know. There is no common thread of information that you can trace back to your experiences with the subject you're having an insight about—rather, you're given information about the true nature of something, and it is up to you to trust it or test out that insight in reality. Given this flash of insight, it's usually a surprise and occurs in an unpredictable way. If the information does not come associated with any kind of feeling in the body or emotions, it is quite often a product of the mind. Sometimes your mind can go on a tangent about things that it's fearful of, and it may even seem as though you're having an intuitive insight. However, if you can trace it back to a fear you know you have, you may be experiencing more of a self-fulfilling prophecy than anything else. Again, the Higher Self functions elusively and is generally unpredictable.

Having an understanding of the various aspects of self is good, but to know it and see it in your reality is better. Take survey of the conversations and decisions you've made in the last week; can you spot when each self came out and made a decision? Did you ever have to negotiate between the impulses of your Lower Self and the wisdom of your Middle Self? Did you have a feeling that came from your Higher Self in the past few months that you could not explain, and later found out the reason for? These examples help you to narrow down which self your feelings come from, and with practice, you'll be able to recognize it in the moment that it's happening.

The meditations following in this chapter will integrate all three selves, as most meditations in the book will. However, there is an emphasis on bringing in elements of all three selves into each meditation. How that occurs will be unique to your experience, but take time afterwards to reflect and ponder which self you may have felt the most. This can be done by simply contemplating, or journaling about your experiences.

Gratitude Expansion

Find a comfortable seated position, and begin breathing deeply to relax.

Once settled, start by giving gratitude to the things immediately surrounding you: be grateful for the floor that supports you, the air you're breathing, and so on. All things that are in your immediate vicinity of which you can be grateful for.

After a few minutes of this, expand your 'bubble of gratitude' out further: find gratitude for the building you're in, things in the room/space you're in, etc. Stay here for a while.

Expand your bubble once again even bigger, maybe as big as the property you're on or city that you're in. Continue in the same fashion as before, going bigger and bigger until all of the Earth has been in your bubble, and then the entire material universe. Spend a comfortable amount of time on each level.

Once gratitude has been given for the entirety of existence, give thanks to the divine force that orchestrated everything in the first place.

Then, most importantly, give thanks to yourself.

Give gratitude for showing up for yourself, meditating, and anything and everything else you can think of to be grateful for that you have done or are doing.

After doing this for as long as feels comfortable, gently drift back into your physical body and ground yourself.

7 Chakra Healing

For this meditation you'll work each chakra individually, all the way up to the 7th using mantras. Don't worry if the following mantras don't resonate with you yet, repeating them helps you build and heal the relationship you have with each chakra.

Using the Dhyani mudra (page x), sit upright and begin by taking slow, deep breathes, focusing your attention inward. Take a few moments to let go of the day, release any thoughts that may be lingering in your mind, and feel the movement of your breath as it enters and leaves your body.

Once relaxed, begin to focus your energy and attention into your first chakra, located at the base of your spine.

While focusing your energy and breathing energy in and out of each chakra, take about three minutes to repeat the following mantras to your chakras individually:

1st Chakra: I am safe. I am safe to explore the world around me. My needs are met, and I am taken care of.

2nd Chakra: I connect with others. I am creative. I am sexual. I connect with those around me socially and beyond.

3rd Chakra: I have personal power over my decisions. I meet any task at hand. I am powerful.

4th Chakra: I connect with others. I love and accept love. I have a healthy relationship with my emotions.

5th Chakra: I speak my truth. I say what needs to be said. I listen to other people's truth without losing mine.

6th Chakra: I can clearly perceive my life. I'm aware of myself and my feelings, and I'm aware of my true deep nature. I am lucid, aware, and awake in this body.

7th Chakra: I am connected with all things. The divine channels through me. I am its vessel. Source is deeply connected through me.

Take a mental note of any blockages or resistance you may have felt that can be worked on later.

Reground your energy, picturing it falling back down through your body and into the earth as though it's planting roots. Once grounded, relax and reflect on your experience.

Power Through Connecting

Begin by breathing deeply and relaxing. Focus your attention on the 3rd chakra (your belly/solar plexus). Build energy into it through intention, and by breathing directly into it.

Next, connect with all things around you through your power center. Imagine your 3rd chakra is a vital piece in all things happening around you, like a plant that is a keystone species within its ecosystem, or a spider spinning its web.

As you connect deeper, allow desire for control to slip away with the realization that true power comes from connection and unity, not dominance.

Allow your will to be transmuted into the divine will, surrendering fully into working together. Let your power become one, and allow your connection with the divine and world around you to guide you into right action, and making decisions with clarity and integrity.

Recognize that the greater good is the wave that change is carried on, and you must surrender to it in order to flow with it.

See that true power comes from allowing divine will or right action to flow through you.

Once you feel complete, reground into the body and conclude the meditation.

4

Childhood Healing

If you made it through your childhood unscathed with no trauma, harsh feelings, or disappointment, congratulations. Kudos to your parents as well—you are perhaps 1-in-a-million.

For the other 99.9999% of us, we have work to do.

Having endured struggle is not a misfortune, but rather a gift. It is your traumas and misfortunes that give you compassion, empathy, and an understanding of what the people around you may be facing. They enable you to comfort the people you love in a way that would not be possible otherwise. Most of all, these experiences open up a vault of wisdom that helps you understand human nature and what people need in times of hardship.

The need to face these past experiences head-on cannot be understated. They do not "go away" with the passage of time, but rather get buried under passing experience. They become embedded deep within our psychology. By facing them directly, we enable ourselves to accept and release these traumas so they no longer subconsciously govern how we behave.

Meditation is not a replacement for therapy; however it is a tremendous aid. With a therapeutic approach to meditation (such as those following in this chapter) you can experience a profound healing of your wounds that you may have held onto your entire life.

It is no secret that oftentimes we carry with us throughout our lives childhood wounds and traumas. They appear in different ways throughout our relationships, ways of engaging with the world around us, our confidence, and so much more. Though it is common to think a trauma is in the past it often appears in our everyday lives in ways that may fool you initially. However, upon closer examination you will begin to see where these things are affecting you, and how they tie back to the original moment of experience. Take for example the lieutenant sniper, Navy SEAL, NASA astronaut, and physician Jonathan Kim. He accomplished more prestige in his various careers than most families do in an entire generation and is considered your typical American badass. Yet his driving force that led him to such heights of ambition and pushing the human body (by his own words) came from him trying to soothe the scared little boy inside of him. Due to a childhood trauma that made him feel powerless, he developed this complex that if he became the best at whatever profession he was in, and when he became the toughest person on the battlefield, this broken inner child would somehow be healed. After becoming a lieutenant, becoming a physician, and becoming a NASA astronaut he found that he could not have been more wrong. Why is this?

It seems as though when we are doing so much to soothe and heal our inner child through these actions that we should be able to "get over" the things that scarred us in the past. Yet, paradoxically, by doing these actions to heal the inner child through indirect means, we could actually be strengthening the wound rather than strengthening the part of us that does the healing.

Childhood healing is something that has to occur directly in order to create real lasting change. This is why therapy is so important and so powerful. You have a professional, and hopefully somebody you trust, to help guide you through your childhood wounds and create a tangible action plan in order to face, address, and accept what happened to you. At the same time they should be providing space to move on and create a meaningful positive life going forward.

So, what does it mean to heal the inner child? It means to integrate this part of yourself that has been hurt, to accept it back into your consciousness, and to move forward acting as one. By acting as one, I mean not giving weight to one part of ourselves (healed) over the other (wounded) when making decisions. It's important to integrate both the healed and the hurt parts of ourselves when making a decision if we are to grow and integrate ourselves into wholeness.

Often people have an ideal that they strive to act from; one of being a totally enlightened being that makes decisions compassionately or strongly without falter. The reality is that when one acts totally from an ideal self instead of their present self, they neglect opportunities that could bring their hurt selves closer to oneness. The end result is swinging back and forth between making smart decisions and feeling like you're fully in alignment, to making impulsive decisions from your hurt self that you regret later. This is the difference between the Higher and Lower Selves mentioned in chapter 3, and why it's important to find balance by making your home in the Middle Self. This too is where childhood healing will take place.

Prior to facing your childhood traumas or pain, you have a part of yourself that is perpetually stuck in the moment of that experience. The consciousness that experienced the trauma, if re-pressed or not looked at, never has time to fully develop with the rest of you. The reason for this is that when you sink into that level of consciousness once again, you pick back up where you left off; which was the moment of trauma. You re-experience that hurt and, most of the time, are unwilling to stay in that space to reconcile your inner child (save you have the specific intention to do so). It is unnatural to willingly stay in a thought we have trained ourselves to suppress, so this comes as no surprise.

But the moment that you choose to stay with that child (or any moment in your life that needs healing) something magical happens. Once the overwhelming wave of emotion subsides from revisiting that moment, you have the opportunity to speak directly to your inner child from the perspective of your current wisdom. You're able to give your inner child the love that they didn't receive, the support they may have lacked, and the understanding that they so desperately needed. From this point, you are able to reconcile that inner child and allow that time of your life to re-enter your consciousness.

Often one singular trauma or sets of trauma can block out years of experiences from your memory. But the truth is those years of fragmented memory are not actually defined by your trauma—only the mind seems to believe that. It is much more likely that during the time of your trauma you also had victories and tremendous learning. Maybe you made a friend that has stuck with you, learned a new skill or hobby, or even simply just had fun participating in whatever was close by. In any case, these moments of anguish do not define the time period that they occurred in. Did they happen? Yes, they did. But do they have to be the end-all-be-all of that chapter of your life? Of course not.

When we heal the inner child, we get to reclaim all of those good memories that happened around that time in our life. Suddenly things become clearer, and though we may have underwent tragedy, there were so many other pockets of light in our lives that are worth appreciating. When these components of our past are given equal weight as our traumatic experiences, the scale of perspective usually tips. At the very best, we can recognize that life wasn't all that bad after all. At worst, we find that even in the darkest of times we can find one or two things to smile at.

From my experience of facilitating childhood healing workshops over the years, this is an incredibly empowering journey. Healing the inner child happens in real time—when we go back and give them the support they needed, a weight is immediately lifted off of our shoulders. You may also be more joyous and playful. That wounded child is given permission to exist within us, and that permission through confronting your traumas is one of the greatest gifts you can ever give yourself in this lifetime.

It is for that reason that I find these following meditations to be the most powerful in this book. They are not the most flashy, do not take you out of your body, and are not tremendous in terms of feeling substantial amounts of energy coursing through your body. But what they do provide is lasting healing. They help us accept parts of ourselves we did not even realize we were denying and create newfound peace that cannot be overturned. If you are look-ing for meditations to quickly help you find harmony again, these are the ones.

But that is not to say that this will be an easy endeavor. Likely while reading this chapter a few memories of yours may have briefly come to mind. The most fleeting of memories that come to mind are often the most powerful—you already know which of your experi-ences have had the biggest impact, and work can be done there too. But there are usually a few sneaky memories that got normalized over the years that may have not been so normal. These experiences, especially those rationalized as just a part of life, are the ones that usually need healing the most.

So spend some time on these meditations. The work will not be completed all in one sitting, or when you finish meditating. They start the internal dialog that leads to healing and lay a very firm foundation for you to do so. The act that you're reading this chapter is enough to prove to yourself you care and are ready to face—and heal—these parts of yourself. So sink into your practice, be brave, and see it through to its end. They could become one of the greatest gifts you ever give to yourself.

Child-Self Healing

This meditation starts with heart breathing (opening up the chest through breathing directly into the heart space, bringing energy directly into the heart). Once in the heart, work backwards in time, through each phase or stage of your life. Maybe you break phases of your life by the years they occurred, the activities you engaged in, or something else that works for you.

Start at the most recent important phase of your life. Recall it and all of the feelings that are associated with it.

At each stage, allow yourself to feel deeply the prominent feelings you experienced during that time of your life. Accept them to your fullest capacity.

Once you have fully accepted these feelings, move into the next stage going backwards in time until you reach the childhood self that first became self-aware of your feelings, desires, and personality. Connect with this childhood self, and tell them anything your heart feels it needs to tell them. Then ask them how they feel, and what they have to say.

Let them speak to you freely as much as they need.

When they are finished, visualize yourself hugging them with so much love that that you begin to melt into each other—you begin to become one. In this deep embrace, you are allowing yourself to become whole again. You are reclaiming these parts of your body and soul. Let this childhood self into your awareness and let it live within your soul, giving you their child-like wisdom and guidance in the moments that you need it most.

When you feel called and the process feels complete, gently come out of meditation, giving yourself some time to reflect on how you feel and what happened.

Inner Child Reiki

For this meditation no specific mudra or meditation position is required. For me, palms facing down over the knees works best. But do what feels natural. Just find yourself comfortable, alert, and ready.

Relax, breathe, and allow your body and mind to come to rest.

Once you've entered into a meditative state and have a sense of clarity, allow yourself to be taken back to the first area, time, and place that comes to mind from your childhood. If nothing comes up, then gently bring yourself back to a moment in your childhood that needs healing.

Hold space with your childhood self, hug them, and tell them how beautiful they are and give them any loving advice they need to hear.

After a while of holding space with this inner child, back out of the scene as if you can see the entire environment. Send loving, healing energy into this whole space. Fill it with love as water would fill a vase.

Once the room is filled with love, send loving energy specifically to your childhood self.

Imagine beautiful, healing energy coming from the earth below your younger self and infusing into their whole body, nourishing them in all the ways they need.

Now imagine them connecting with radiant, healing white light energy coming from above them, offering the same love and guidance from the heavens.

Finally, after this energy has been infused with your childhood self, recollect all of the accomplishments you've had since you were this age and tell your younger self all about them.

Reflect and give gratitude for all of these amazing changes and growth. Give yourself a moment to feel joy and be proud of all of the work you've done and thank your childhood self for getting through the difficult moments to bring you to this point.

Once you feel satisfied with your meditation, ground back into your senses. Be gentle returning to your day and take time to reflect.

5

Moving the Energy

If you've ever taken a yoga class, done a guided meditation, or have had an extended conversation about either, there's a good chance you've heard of your chakras. This chapter will explain each of your main seven chakras in brief detail, because they're an important reference point when talking about spiritual energy.

Though this chapter is going to be jam-packed with information, don't get too lost in the details. Again, it serves as a reference point, so don't let it distract you from the *actual experience* of meditating.

To give you an idea of how the chakras may play out in your experience with life or meditation, let's start with a story. It will hopefully illuminate how working on a single chakra can shift the trajectory of your life before moving into the meat of the subject.

It was 2020, and I had just exited a hot mess of a relationship. My partner and I didn't like each other on a fundamental level, intimacy just wasn't there, but we were blinded by the mutual attachment that we had developed towards one another. Prior to this relationship, I had spent about 2 years celibate without much social interaction... so to be coming out of a relationship without intimacy after years of celibacy was disheartening, to say the least.

I knew prior to the relationship I had some serious blocks in my 2nd chakra (associated with sexuality, creativity, and being social) going back to childhood. If I was going to overcome them, I knew it was going to take some serious work.

So after that partnership I set my intention to heal my relationship with my own sexuality—a journey that ironically happens by yourself, in the privacy of your own thoughts and body.

I began listening to guided meditations focusing on healing the 2nd chakra, combing YouTube for talks about it, and doing my own meditations to see what was happening inside to make me have apprehension towards connecting with others.

Each time I went into meditation exploring my own feelings towards intimacy, I discovered more pieces to the puzzle. I noticed that I had a lingering pain in my lower back, and I had grown so accustomed to it that I never made the connection between the pain and what energy center it was located in. I noticed that I couldn't visualize the color orange so well in my 2nd chakra, which is the color that it resonates at. Most of all, I saw that when I visualized making love with someone my body reacted in a flinch more than it welcomed the possibility. The last aspect was a telling one.

Remembering that trauma is stored in the body, I began examining my past to figure out where the association was created between sex and feeling threatened. That's when it dawned on me: all the times I gave up my power and had sex with an ex-partner who I wasn't comfortable with or truly attracted to did not come without consequence—in fact my body had not gotten over it at all. It was too easy to be passive and let it happen. Yet years later, those experiences were still locked within the area of my hips and were affecting everything I did. I saw it in everything from my relationships, to stretching, down to what foods I chose to enjoy. It became clear that my short-comings in my most recent relationship were tied to this feeling of still feeling threatened by someone I had not seen in years, and it was causing me actual physical pain in my lower back to hold onto.

In response, I began doing many of the meditations listed in this book: using the childhood healing meditation to give myself the support I needed, using the white light chakra healing to clear old energy, breathing with the Earth to calm myself down, and even more meditations that happened spontaneously. The common thread was that they all focused on feeling peace in my pelvic area, replacing old energy with new vibrant orange energy, and uncovering everything stored in that part of the body that needed to be addressed.

Amazingly enough, as I worked through the blockage on the inside, the world around me started to warp and help me grow on the outside too. Of the most amazing events that took place around that time, I had the opportunity to confront the ex-partner that created much of the blockage I was experiencing. Coincidentally, she was visiting Florida after spending the last few years on the other side of the country and was interested in catching up.

Without me even mentioning it, she apologized for all of the times she pressured me into having sex with her. That simple gesture gave me tremendous healing—not only did it give me reassurance that it was safe to connect with others again, but it reconciled the parts of me that were still holding on to that trauma. Parts of me that I didn't even know needed to be healed.

I was able to recognize clearly that my fears were not attached to intimacy, but to her past self that would pressure me to have sex in order to give her some sense of validation. By working on my meditations and trying to heal the 2nd chakra, I was given one of the most healing opportunities of all: the chance to forgive, simply through circumstance. In doing so, I was able to regain the key components of trust and safety in my relationships with others.

This theme continued even beyond that interaction. There was another relationship in my life that carried a similar pattern, and circumstances led to me confronting that person too. Though this time there was no real apology or reassurance from the other party, confronting them allowed me to take full responsibility for the healing that was left to do and begin doing that work. Though the person could not fully acknowledge the consequences of consistently ignoring my boundaries, the confrontation set me free, and my meditations kept getting deeper with my 2nd chakra.

I finally began reaching a point where the pain in my 2nd chakra wasn't there everyday, and my apprehension towards intimacy was fading. I had been focusing my meditations on this specific chakra for a few months, and the difference was amazing. I began feeling comfortable in large groups again, and I felt safe casually flirting with people I found attractive. I wasn't quite comfortable being physically intimate with someone yet, but the unearthing and facing my trauma had freed me more than I could have imagined.

After a while of dipping my toes into the waters of intimacy, my meditations began to point that it was time to get out there and test my lessons against the anxiety of connecting with others. It was at this time that I finally stumbled upon someone I felt comfortable with. We met at a festival in the middle of nowhere, and we happened to have a lot of similarities. We did the same kinds of art, liked similar music, and more importantly experienced similar kinds of struggles with being confident in our partnerships. Together we were able to work on these things slowly. Because we knew each other's past, taking our time to heal and hold each other accountable was the only natural thing to do. That relationship blossomed into a beautiful time of growth and healing for us both, pushing us forward into understanding what we wanted out of a relationship.

It was less about our partner, but more about what we wanted out of ourselves. It seemed as though the last year of meditating had finally come to fruition. All of the time spent sifting through my feelings alone was being actualized in front of me as how I interacted with others. The work in my 2nd chakra that seemed insurmountable just a year prior had become mostly complete, and I felt comfortable engaging in partnerships and dealing with things as they came up.

I reached a level of healing and growth that would have been unimaginable, simply by focusing my energy and intentions towards healing the chakra governing sexuality. Things that I thought were unavoidable character traits of mine had been worked through and released so that a new me could take form. Of all the gifts I could have received from meditation, this is perhaps one of the greatest. Growth and transformation into a fuller, healthier version of myself.

I share that story to make relevant the healing power that comes from knowing the following information. If you don't know much about your chakras, pay attention to this chapter. Within it contains information that can be applied to many aspects of your life today.

The word chakra means wheel, and you have seven major energy points or chakra wheels positioned throughout your body. Think of them as energetic organs or even a sixth sense. Each chakra is responsible for interpreting a different aspect of reality and your experience within it. This will be explained in more detail with each chakra.

The seven chakras run up from the base of your spine to the crown of your head, and each one is associated with a different kind of experience, and a different color. Following is a summary of each chakra: it's associated color, it's main intersection with your life experiences, how to know when it's blocked, and how to heal it. Each of the following chakras can be healed through yoga, meditation, and any other mindful practice; however, there are a few tips on how to remedy any blockage quickly through your actions.

1st chakra- Starting from the bottom up your first chakra is known as your root chakra. It's located at the base of your spine and the color associated with it is red. This energy center has everything to do with your survival instincts, having a roof over your head, and feeling comfortable in the reality you're in.

How to know when it's blocked: Generally, when this chakra is blocked you will either experience pain at the point of your 1st vertebrae, or struggle with passing stool. Think about any time that you've slept over at a friend's house for the first time; I know it's silly to notice, but you probably didn't poop. When you feel out of your physical place of comfort, this chakra is the one most affected.

How to unblock this chakra: Take care of your body and environment! Go for a barefoot walk in the grass, clean your space, eat healthy (especially root vegetables if available), exercise, and focus on solving any looming situations that affect your home, health, or finances. Meditation can help, but this chakra is all about connecting physically and harmoniously with the reality you're in.

2nd chakra- The second chakra is located right in the area of your pelvis. This is the energy center of sexuality, creativity & self-expression, and your ability to connect with other human beings. The color associated with this energy center is orange.

How to know when it's blocked: You will experience lower back pain, have issues in your sex life, and have creative blockages when energy is not flowing here correctly. You also may feel isolated and alone.

How to unblock this chakra: Embrace your creativity and sensuality. Allow yourself to be flirty, share consensual touch with others (platonically is just as sufficient), paint, sing, or dance, and eat foods that make your heart sing. Anything that you can take healthy pleasure in is going to help you feel safe in opening up this chakra.

3rd chakra- The third chakra located right in the area of your navel. The color associated with it is yellow, and this one has to do with your personal power, your confidence, your self-assertion, and overall your presence when you enter a room and establish yourself. This chakra is known as your power center due to the nature of the items mentioned. In addition, it is also your psychic center (ever have a gut feeling?).

How to know when it's blocked: You may have trouble digesting, loss of appetite, or even stomach pains. Emotionally, you may be dealing with depression or a lack of control in your life.

How to unblock this chakra: Step into your power! If this chakra is blocked, it's likely due to not speaking your truth and letting your boundaries get crossed. Notice where in your life you may be walked on or giving away your power, and let go of those situations in the healthiest way possible. Be vocal about how you feel, set your boundaries, and don't accept or act on anything outside of your integrity.

4th chakra- The fourth chakra is your heart center. It connects you with your emotions and is responsible for loving the people around you, the life around you, what you do, and engaging with life in general with joy. All of your deepest feelings in everyday life are usually housed in the 4th chakra. The color associated with this chakra is green. It's important to note as well that this chakra is right in the middle—you have three chakras going down below it and three chakras above, so your heart center is actually your integration point between those two worlds. This is where all of the big work usually happens for us, and this especially is where we can transcend the scenarios we've been facing and move onto the next lesson. It's the most spiritually connected aspect of our Middle Self.

How to know when it's blocked: Mid-back pains, chest pains, and heaviness of the shoulders are among the most common physical signs. In addition, you may not be feeling as many emotions, as though your emotional pallet has been made dull. You also may have trouble feeling empathy and compassion for others.

How to unblock this chakra: Practice gratitude. Find anything that you're grateful for, and expand on it. The Gratitude Expansion meditation on page 28 is great for opening this chakra back up. Do things you genuinely love, and if you have anyone in your life that you love, call them. Remembering these simple loving connections can be an energetic defibrillator to get you back on track.

5th chakra- The fifth chakra (or throat chakra) is associated with our ability to recognize and tell our truth, to express ourselves, and be vocal about what we're feeling. The color associated with this chakra is a light blue. If you ever have a moment where you feel pressure in your throat right before exclaiming your truth, you're feeling the physical stimulation of energy being focused in the fifth chakra.

How to know when it's blocked: You may quite literally feel as though you're being choked up, or have returning neck pains. This could last but a moment, or years depending on how quickly you act on correcting what is causing the blockage. Beyond the physical, you may have trouble speaking your truth or feel anxiety about speaking up in situations in your life.

How to unblock this chakra: Speak your truth, and accept your truth. If this chakra is blocked, you are likely either A) not speaking up to someone about what you've been feeling, or B) having trouble accepting the reality of a situation or your feelings about it.

Speak up to the parties involved until you feel complete—that even includes yourself.

6th chakra- The sixth chakra is associated with your ability to perceive truth and your ability to see clearly. It's also known as your third eye center for this reason. The color associated with this chakra is an indigo or deep blue, and when you hear people say they're "opening their 3rd eye," this is the energy center that they're referring to.

How to know when it's blocked: You may not seem to recognize signs and patterns as they are happening to you. You can no longer predict what may come next in the situations you face, and make mistakes you normally wouldn't. Your mood may also swing more or easier than normal. Physically, this blockage can appear through headaches that feel concentrated on the center of your forehead.

How to unblock this chakra: Practice visualization, and slow yourself down enough to contemplate and assess the situations in your life. Think of this chakra as a body of water—if you want to use it clearly, you have to wait for the debris to settle and be momentarily undisturbed. Create quiet time and journal so you can try and see things from a new or different perspective.

7th chakra- Your seventh chakra, or crown chakra, is located right at the top of your skull. This energy center is associated with your connection with the divine, the universe, and everything encompassed in that. This is the portal or gateway when you do things like astral projecting (leaving your body) or go through a near-death experience. The seventh chakra is your exit point in these cases. The color associated with this energy center is usually either a lavender color or white.

How to know when it's blocked: You do not feel a connection with anything around you—as though you're a foreign, alien specimen walking around in a dead material world. You may also struggle with learning new things, and depression. Physically, you may be more easily affected by sensitivity to light.

How to unblock this chakra: Meditate, meditate, meditate. Being mindful, and focusing your attention on the crown of your head is the most direct way to solve this blockage. Try to see the connections between yourself and nature—contemplate how both you and trees use the same patterns to carry nutrients (roots and veins). Focusing on how your being is reflected in nature can help, but meditation is really what does the trick on this one.

So now you have a functioning understanding of the chakras, and a guide to fall back on when you know you're feeling stuck. Often times when a physical ailment appears, there were signs that appeared prior if it is related to an imbalance in your energy. Things usually first appear as energetic blockages, then emotional unbalance/blockages, then lastly as physical pains and tension.

The deeper you dive into your meditation practice, the more adept you will become at catching these blockages before they become physical. With practice, you'll be able to sense the energetic or emotional blockage in the moment that it happens. Pay attention to patterns in your life, especially areas in your body where you consistently feel unexplained tension. What energy center is this located near? Is there something you can take away from the experience?

As you move through the rest of the book, pay close attention to anywhere in your body that cannot come into full relaxation when meditating—especially when the rest of your body is at rest.

During meditation is the easiest time to catch a glimpse of possible blockages before they become physical, giving yourself the opportunity to work on things as fluidly as they may come.

Future Self Visualization

Begin by breathing and finding your center as you relax, preparing for a journey of visualization.

Next, begin visualizing something that you've been craving in your recent life; a reality that you truly, deeply want in your heart.

Imagine every detail of it, as crisply as you can. See the reality that it is placed in, the entirety of the setting, the colors, textures, and physical items.

Once you see it as if it were right in front of you, focus on the sensation of it being in your hands/reality and all of the emotions that come with that.

Fully be there, in that reality, with everything that you want. As you see it clearly, realize that what you're seeing and experiencing already exists in the future.

Connect with this reality even deeper, affirming that it's already in existence and just has yet to be manifested.

Invite your future self into the scene, and connect even deeper with the details of what you're seeing.

Ask your future self and the reality you're seeing what you can do to further make yourself ready for that reality. Ask for any advice in order to help you more fluidly enter that reality, and truly believe that it is coming. Advice can come in words, feelings, images, or intuitively.

Give gratitude for your future self to open up that space and allow you to see into that window of your coming future/reality.

Thank your future self for all of the advice it gave you, and slowly begin drifting back to your body, grounding yourself in your physical senses before opening your eyes.

Releasing With Intention

Find a comfortable seated position and begin by deeply breathing. Focus on the feeling of your breath as it enters and leaves your body, and the way you feel in the current moment.

Release any thoughts from your day and simply relax.

Once you feel yourself falling deeper into meditation, notice any blockages or areas to be worked on in your body.

Once you've identified these areas, imagine you can move your "spirit arms" without moving your physical arms. You can see them made of light, and you use them to push out your blockage out of your body and in front of you.

Take time to continue pushing any blockages out of your body, and visualize that they are in front of you, but not connected to you.

Look at them and see them intuitively, letting the blockages tell you what they are and what is causing them.

Ask yourself how to replace this energy. Let your feelings guide you in doing so, and once the energy is replaced let the blockages go, free to become one with the earth and recycled into something new.

When you're ready to end the meditation, begin to become aware again of your bodily sensations and how you physically feel in this moment. Feel your breath expanding your chest.

Once you're re-grounded, open your eyes and reflect.

Full Circle Healing

Begin by relaxing, slowing down the breath, and preparing for a visual journey.

Picture the Divine's energy right in front of you. For you it may appear as white light, an aura surrounding a deity, or something else entirely. Take energy from the divine (or advice/insight, etc.) into the left side of your body, moving through you and entering into any chakras or parts of the body that have been giving you trouble.

Inhale divine energy and healing to these parts, and exhale giving the energy back to the Divine.

After running energy through those areas, bring the energy to the heart, then back to the problem area, and let it circle back out of the body to the right and into the Divine.

Allow yourself to open up to the love, guidance, advice, and healing that the Divine is giving to you. Use any intentions you have and communicate them.

When you feel like your cup is full and you've received all you need, gently come back to the body and reground yourself.

6

Integration

The purpose of life is not to master meditating, but rather the purpose of meditating is to master life. Undoubtedly, the most important factor in doing so is our ability to integrate our meditation experiences into our everyday life. A life full of deep moments in the quiet of your bedroom is great, but ultimately does not have much value if it cannot be made applicable to one's own life.

One factor of how you can integrate your experiences better is coming back to your everyday reality with the acceptance of who and what you are. Feeling comfortable in one's skin and life is of the utmost importance. Meditation can bring you many things, but being at peace with your life is one of the best benefits. Finding a deeper sense of acceptance of your reality creates an echo chamber that fuels deeper meditations. These meditations lead to deeper peace and acceptance, which leads to better meditations, and so on. This compounding effect is what not only leads to a much happier life, but also the more sensational aspects of meditation that people are fascinated by.

Oftentimes people are interested in pursuing meditation to open their 3rd eye, deepen their intuition, and in some cases astral project (leave their body). Some common phrases one might here from someone with these motivations to meditate are: "I'll understand things when my 3rd eye is open;" "once my heart is fully open I'll be ready for a partner;" "I'll be at peace once I figure out what all these things in my life mean;" "Astral projection sounds so cool!"

These statements aren't fundamentally wrong, but the approach to meditation is often crippled by this logic. Instead of fostering peace, these motivations operate on the assumption that there is something wrong with you now, or that life as it stands is dull and useless, and meditation will cure you of the diagnosis of being born. This could not be further from the truth.

Though you absolutely can achieve all of the things mentioned and more through meditation, the path will be much slower if your practice is viewed as a solution, or a means to an end.

Meditation is a tool, not an end-all problem solver. It provides clarity, removes anxiety, and gives confidence to seize opportunities in your life as they appear. But ultimately, when it's time to apply the lessons and insights that came from your practice, action must be made in your everyday life.

Profound insight can come from meditation, but profound transformation comes from how you use those insights to better your relationship with your life and the world around you. Thinking that you can solve your problems and transform yourself solely with meditation is a trap.

At first it will likely feel as though you are progressing at an incredible rate, and meditation can seem like the answer to all your problems... but then you plateau. The same is true with any new skill or practice you develop, such as skateboarding, swimming, or yoga. However, meditation is unique in the sense that you won't just stop progressing rapidly, but you may stop making any progress all together. It's not because you are bad at meditating, and it's certainly not because meditation just isn't for you. Instead, it's because meditation is preparation for living life, not a bypass. In order to continue diving deeper into your practice, you must be living your everyday life with the meditative wisdom you've gained. There will be many trials, and even more knocks to your ego. You'll have times where you think you have it all figured out, and periods of feeling as though you'll never be sure about anything in life ever again. These experiences can be taxing on the mind and heart, but it's important to remember that you are not either of these extremes; you are how you deal with them.

This means that you cannot define yourself by your lows—but at the same time, you cannot define yourself solely on the love and light of your peaks. You are the Middle: the negotiator between the two. You are how you handle and interpret this experience.

Your nature comes from beyond: a limitless, infinite potential of energy and possibilities. But one does not incarnate into a human vessel to just explore the astrals, lose themselves in the higher energies, and totally transcend known reality. Nor is it to fully lose oneself in the events happening around us, being swung mercilessly by life's circumstances. Though we can and do hit these peaks and valleys, bringing back the wisdom from these experiences is what is important.

You came to be human, so be human. Take the lesson, take the miracles, take the mind-bending experiences and use them to your human advantage. Help others who are along the path, in whatever form you can.

We are all geniuses in our own right, and there is something we can do better than many people around us. If that something can give you joy, then pursue it. It will be your gift to the planet. Allow your meditations to aid you in this quest, as there is no greater purpose than dumping your gifts and insights into the collective consciousness to better the world.

You are infinite, there is no question to this. But you are also human, and equally so this is your reality for the time being. Trying to escape it through meditation practices and sensational experience is not just a waste of time, but a squandering of an incredible opportunity to be human. Let your practice ground you, and let it guide you. But understand it will never contain all of the answers, even if it feels as though it would. When you hit your plateau, that's the sign you've been waiting for that answers will come to you through experience. Your stagnation is a call that you must be brave and face the world.

This is what integration is all about. This does not mean dropping meditation—but rather finding a balance between how much you rely on insights through meditation, and how much learning you can generate through the trial and error of trying things out.

A major trap that can befall even the most earnest of spiritual seekers is waiting until you are totally clear before making a decision or action. Even with the utmost level of intuition and spiritual practice, the stars will never be perfectly aligned for you to jump into an opportunity or venture. You will never have all the answers prior to making your leap. Sometimes looking back it may feel as though you did, but this is just a misperception—if you felt like you had all the answers before a decision, you didn't. You simply had enough synchronicities happen for you to have the courage to act on your faith.

The more you practice meditation, the greater your faith will deepen. You will see the universe is working for you and through you, not just around you.

But it takes tremendous patience to get there. Rome wasn't built in a day, but it was built by men and women who could not see the full future of what their efforts would mean a millennia later. They acted on faith, conviction, and the belief that what they were doing had purpose. Your life, accomplishments, and trajectory are no different.

In the grand scheme of things, we are really here to learn and experience what it is like to be human. Not for the sake of being better at something else after this life, but for the sake of itself. There is tremendous value and joyful experience from being present with who you are and what you want, and then acting on that information.

Let your meditations guide you into knowing yourself. Let them be full and rich, as well as foggy and lame. Let them show you the limitlessness of the universe, and the infinite detail in a single atom. But more than anything, let them prepare you for your life, and bring you to the edge of what you feel your human purpose is.

When the time comes to leap off the edge that life has brought you to, leap. Everything in the universe has led you there... and more importantly, who knows what's waiting on the other side?

Integrate your meditation experiences, and let them help you live a better life. Meditation is not a substitute for life, but its enhancement. So take the book in stride as a resource, but never stop learning.

These last two meditations are some of my personal favorites when it comes to healing and growth. I hope that they, along with the other meditations in the book, contribute in a meaningful way to your path in meditation and beyond.

White Light Chakra Healing

Begin by breathing and relaxing, preparing for deeper meditation with your hands in the Dhyana mudra (page x).

Starting from the top down (or bottom up if you'd like) imagine healing white light over each of the chakras. Connect with it, let it heal you and your energy centers, realigning them to a state of balance.

After going through each chakra, let white light expand into the entire body. Notice any pain or blockages that come up.

Work on these blockages for a few minutes, and when you feel your work is complete, reground yourself and engage the senses.

Trust Yourself

Find a comfortable seated position and begin by deeply breathing. Focus on the feeling of your breath as it enters and leaves your body, and the way you feel in the current moment.

Release any thoughts from your day and simply relax.

Focus on breathing into your heart, expanding your heart chakra center and feeling it deeply. Affirm to yourself, "I trust myself." It's ok to have self-doubt when beginning this process.

Keep repeating this affirmation inside yourself until you can literally feel the part of you that trusts yourself, even if it's a small part of you.

Once you've felt this part of you, breathe into that part of you, giving it energy and helping it grow.

Do so for as long as necessary and ground yourself back into your body when you feel the meditation is complete.

About the Author

Gordon Rojo has been a meditation facilitator since 2017, leading group journeys and meditating every day for eight years. Starting from the age of 17, Gordon set himself up on a course to understand what consciousness was, how it operates, and how it could be adapted to live a happier life. Immersing himself in Buddhist styles of meditation, Qi Gong, Zen mindfulness, alongside many methods discovered through his own practice, meditation helped him overcome the grief of a difficult childhood and navigate who he is. Ultimately, meditation helped him understand his passions, his purpose, and how he wanted to show up in the world.

For more, visit DeepHealingMeditations.org